Fingers which Plucks the Star

Translated by
S.Mohan Raj M.A, B.Ed, M.Phil,(Ph.D),M.A, (Yoga)

Aelay Publish

Published By:
Aelay Publish
5/175, Fathima nagar,
Kuthenkuly,
Tirunelveli -627104
Phone: 9944992571

Design And Executed by

ISBN : 978-93-5533-075-8
Page : 117

Content

About the translator

S. Mohan Raj is a Research Scholar at Vellore Institute of Technology (VIT), Vellore, India. He is a budding writer who has published several papers, articles, and poems in conferences. He is active in his research alongside writing. His areas of interest are Indian writing in English, translation studies, cultural studies, comparative literature, and ELT. He currently works on comparative literature and cultural studies. He has presented 55 papers and has published more than 40 papers. He has presented two papers in the conferences held in Malaysia. He has published poems both in Tamil and English, received two awards for poetry writing. He also received the best presenter award and cash award twice. He has delivered two guest talks in the workshops. He has taken Mr. S. Senthilkumar's poetry collection 'விண்மீன் பறிக்கும் விரல்கள்' for the translation. He can be reached at rajmohan251@gmail.com 9751660760.

About the Author

The author of the book '*விண்மீன் பறிக்கும் விரல்கள்*' Mr. Senthilkumar was born in Devikapuram, a small town near Arani. He has completed his schooling in his hometown and has studied under graduation and postgraduation Tamil literature at Thiruppanandal Tamil College. He has worked as a Professor of Tamil in a self-finance college and has participated in more than twenty international and national seminars. He is currently working as a Post Graduate Tamil Teacher in Government Higher Secondary School.

Foreword

இலக்கியம் என்பது ஒரு காலக் கண்ணாடி, இது மனிதர்களின் செயல்களைக் குறித்துப் பதிவு செய்து கொள்ளும் வரலாற்றுப் பெட்டகமாக விளங்குகிறது. தற்காலத்தில் இலக்கியம் மனித வாழ்வில் இன்றியமையாத அங்கமாகி விட்டது. கவிதை பல பரிமாணத்துடன் செழித்து வளரும் இலக்கியப் பிரிவு. இதில் பல வகைகள் இருப்பினும் கவிதைகளில் மொழி பெயர்ப்பு சற்று சவாலான காரியமே. அந்தச் சவாலான காரியத்தைத் தன் கடினமான உழைப்பின் மூலம் சிறப்பாகச் செய்து முடித்துள்ளார் இந்த மொழி பெயர்ப்பு நூலின் ஆசிரியர் முனைவர் பட்ட ஆய்வாளர், கவிஞர் திரு. சீ. மோகன் ராஜ் அவர்கள். அவரின் இந்த மொழி மாற்றக் கவிதை சிறப்பான முறையில் அமைந்துள்ளது. திரு. சீ. மோகன் ராஜ் அவர்களின் தமிழ் ஆர்வத்திற்கும் ஆங்கிலத்தில் அவர் கொண்டுள்ள புலமைக்கும் இந்த நூல் சான்றாக விளங்குகிறது. எதிர் காலத்தில் இவர் இது போல் பல நூல்கள் படைத்து அன்னை தமிழுக்கும் இலக்கிய உலகிற்கும் பெருமை சேர்க்க வேண்டும் என்று மனமார வாழ்த்துகிறேன்.

புலவர் கோ. தணிகைமலை
தலைமையாசிரியர்
அரசு உயர் நிலைப் பள்ளி, சே.கூடலூர்
திருவண்ணாமலை

தம்பி திரு. சீ. மோகன் ராஜ் மிகச் சிறந்த படைப்பாளி, வாசகர், ஆய்வாளர், பேராசிரியர் போன்ற பன்முகம் கொண்டவர். எடுத்துக் கொள்ளும் எந்தச் செயலையும் சீரிய முறையில் முனைப்புடனும் செய்து முடிப்பவர். தன்னடக்கத்திலும் பண்பிலும் சிறந்தவர். என்னுடைய இந்த நூலை மொழிபெயர்த்து எனக்குப் பெருமை சேர்த்திருகின்றார். இவர்க்கு இசைவு தெரிவிப்பதோடு வாழ்த்தி மகிழ்கிறேன்.

சு. செந்தில்குமார்
முதுநிலை தமிழ் ஆசிரியர்
அரசு மேல்நிலைப் பள்ளி, ஒண்ணுபுரம்
திருவண்ணாமலை

Perspectives are always different. Even though there are many versions of our ancient writings, like Thirukkural, Ramayana, Mahabharata, etc., the essence of the Source Language must be tasted by the Target Language readers too. I would like to appreciate Mr. S. Mohan Raj for retaining the freshness and exact essence of the Tamil Poetry into the translated version. Few Tamil words are very hard to translate in English; especially some nouns like (Mullai poo). I wish wholeheartedly that his new avatar as a translator to touch the peak and pluck the stars of victory with his literary fingers.

C. Mohanapriya
Assistant Professor, Department of English
Hindusthan College of Arts and Science
Coimbatore

Literature is one of the factors that help man to be more humane. Literature is a writing form for humans to express their emotions. Translation in modern literature has created a separate reader circle for itself. In particular, various poems have been translated into many languages from the time of the *Sangam* age to the present day. In that regard, this translation by my friend and doctoral researcher Mr. S. Mohan Raj will always remain fresh in my mind. As a first reader of his writing, I convey my hearty congratulations for his literary endeavours.

T. Adalarasu M.A., M. Phil, B.Ed.,
Assistant Professor, Department of English
Bharath Vidhya Mandhir Arts and Science College
Thandarampet, Tiruvannamalai

A word from the Author

Translating a book is a tedious venture that too translating a poetry collection requires a lot of patience. I feel happy that I possess some patience to take my initial step in translation. This book is my tender attempt which brings different worlds and colours. I request the readers to kindly bear if there are any errors and support me for my future works. Thank you.

Acknowledgement

Working on translating a book is harder than I thought and more rewarding than I could have ever imagined. None of this would have been possible without the blessings of God almighty.

I thank my father T. Srinivasan; mother S. Dharani Bai; and brother S. Sundharraj for their continuous moral support. I Would like to thank my beloved wife Mrs.A.Jeevitha Mohan Raj, I thank my maternal Uncle Mr. K.Jayakanthan and family for providing a space to work.

I extend my sincere thanks to my guide and research supervisor Dr. V. Sunitha for her motivation and support.

I thank my friend T. Adalarasu, and my beloved sisters (C. Mohanapriya & M. Gayathri) for their support and I extend my sincere thanks to all who have rendered foreword, whoever motivate me and support me

1. **Aim**

   Lamp
   shows the
   light,
   Aim
   shows you
   in light!

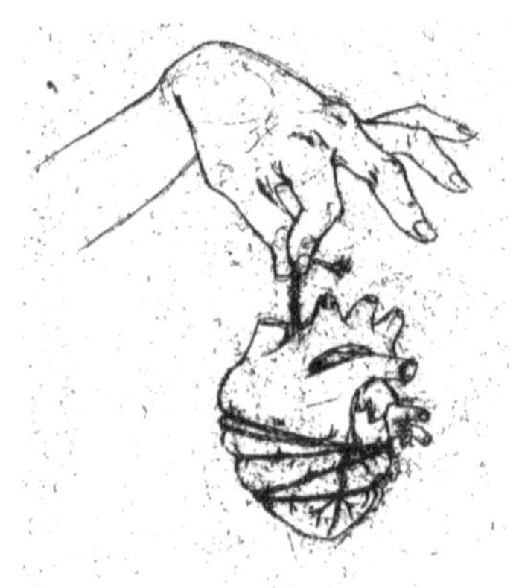

2. **Love**

   Between
   you and me,
   happens a
   heart transplantation
   without pain!

3. **Spring City**

    No more

    paddy fields or trees!

    There stands

    Spring City,

    It welcomes you!

4. **Moon Bindi**

    Which maiden

    wipes her face?

    The sky towel

    sticks with the moon Bindi!

5. **The National Bird**

It went extinct,

the peacocks' count.

You are the national bird!

increased tremendously;

Not mere mosquitoes!

It's an underestimation.

You fertilise diseases and

harvest human lives - indeed

a supreme power you are!

Fingers which Plucks the Star

It is because of your invasion,

free men

enslave themselves

in the nets during the nights!

We clap,

for your music concert

at our ears,

But you take to heels!

Mosquitoes...

though dwelling in drainage

you are also capitalists!

Since, you suck the blood of

poor people!

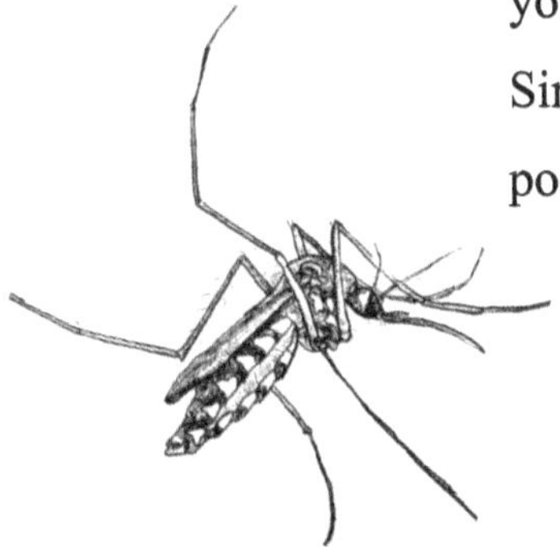

6. **Failures are also a [1]*Yagna***

We fell

while we just began to walk.

It is because of those failures,

we stood up again and we walked!

Don't regret to face

failures - a wild poison –

while churning the trying-sea!

Achieving success is not immediate,

it comes out of labour!

Failures prepare you for success.

But success buys you with price

and sells you to fame!

Keep walking

Let the failures

tells your victories address!

---

[1] *Yogna* – a ritual, involves sacrifice and offerings with specific purpose

together

7. **Then and Now**

Then

We were far away...

Despite

we felt close by!

Now

We are near...

Yet

we feel distant!

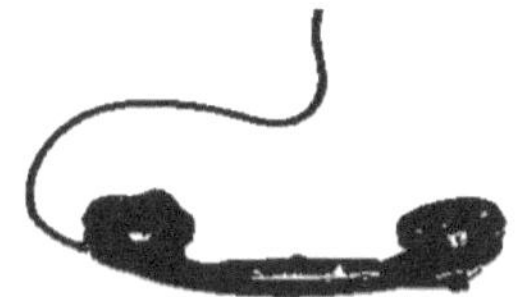

Together but
Separate

8. **Let us Plant Love**

Food - served for stomach cravings;

Love - never served for heart's craving!

People below poverty line are lesser

then the people below love line!

Once,

Mail - as vehicle -

carried love!

Now,

The vehicle is broken down

and love became aged!

[2]Valluvar dedicated

a chapter for love.

Now,

Love caved in

and power beefed up!

"Love is God", said [3]Thirumoolar.

Now,

In heart's coop

love became a corpse!

The heart has four chambers,

Let us make the love to live

at least in one chamber!

Let us plant love,

before the world buried.

Let us yield

the fruit of humanity!

[2] Thiruvalluvar, great Tamil poet commonly known as Valluvar
[3] Tamil Shaivite and writer considered one of the sixty-three
Nayanmars and one of the 18 Siddhars.

9. **Book Feather**

Rather than the mother

carrying the foetus,

You, the bearer of ideas,

identifies a good man to the world!

Thou,

in paper leaves offer

knowledge feast!

Books are feather,

that shows the world!

Spread the book wings,

the Sphere will be visible!

Even,

Valluvar and [4]Kamban

who lived in palm huts,

known to the world

after getting into the book house!

---

[4] Kamban, a great Tamil poet, who wrote Kamba *Ramayana* in the Tamil language

Fingers which Plucks the Star

Computers

preyed humans of this century,

Hence

no human beings were left

to read books!

Oh, People!

You are not even ready

to understand that the

helmet is necessary.

Then how could make you to understand

that books are the

armour of knowledge?

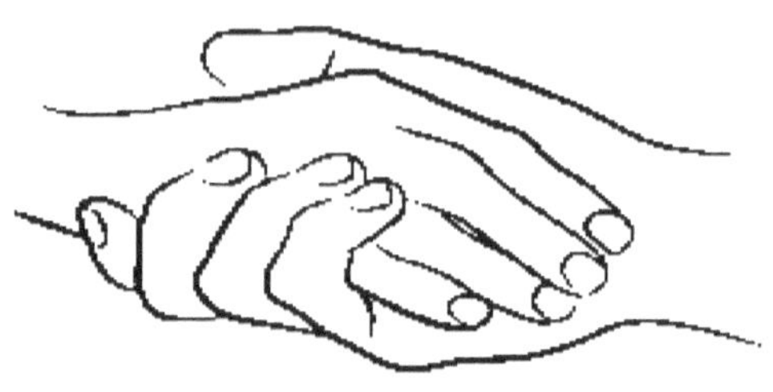

10. **Salvation**

They are not travelling

in life's path,

Their life is travelling

only on the footpaths!

They are human exhibitions,

kept at footpaths as

meaningless poverty's

witnesses!

In this,

a few green leaves wade out

into dried and charred leaves!

Celebrators of Independence Day!

See they are still enslaved,

and are living

under poverty!

The Government is looking for a way

to settle on the moon,

Is there any way for them

to settle in their homes?

Will they get their homes,

at least, after their death?

11. Tree, a being Boon

Thou,

not a tree,

the boon of soil!

Even if you grow up,

you will stand with branches;

We will cut our family branches,

for our growth!

You send wind - a messenger

to the cloud saying your love!

The clouds turn into rain, leaves you drenched,

embrace the soil and flows!

You shed tears in love failure;

the Earth gets aromatic, even at your failure!

Tears are, too heavy, in our love failures!

Do you know why we're cutting you?

Whoever grows up, we don't like!

Don't worry for that you are being chopped

Even though cut down

you are addressed as wood!

But

We are mocked as corpse!

12. **Bharathi, a Great Fire**

When a Sun sprouted

in the soil of Ettayapuram,

Even, the celestial Sun sweats!

In the Indian sky

'White clouds' encompassed,

Indian mother

was curled up with

the hunger of freedom!

Children were gathering

revolutionary firewood

to cook independence,

In which [5]Bharathi

ignited through his poems of fire!

His home stove was off,

but the stomach stove was burning!

Food turned as a mere dream for him,

but the nation's dream has become his food!

Before the freedom thirst quench,

did death get a thirst over Bharathi?

---

[5] Bharathi, Tamil poet, journalist, independence activist, and a social reformer born at Ettayapuram, Tamilnadu

13. **Lips, are Also Literature!**

Your lip lines are

lyrics of literature!

Why are you afraid of my

reading and tasting those lines?

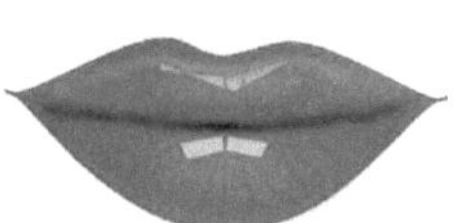

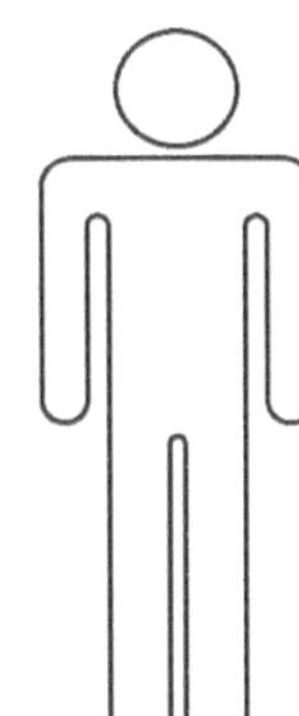

14. **The Ambition**

If

tragedies pass,

heights are at your disposal!

15. **Lord**

The Lord may be in any form,

He who has a heart,

can become a Lord!

16. Non-violence

Despite the head is cut off,

tender coconut offers you water,

- An example for non-violence!

17. Self-confidence

He who knows himself, does not degrade.

He who is self-confident, does not fall!

18. Moon Girl

Oh, Moon Girl!

Don't come out at night,

Look, how many stars there

winking at you!

Don't be afraid,

They will sneak when the sun

comes up with light-rod!

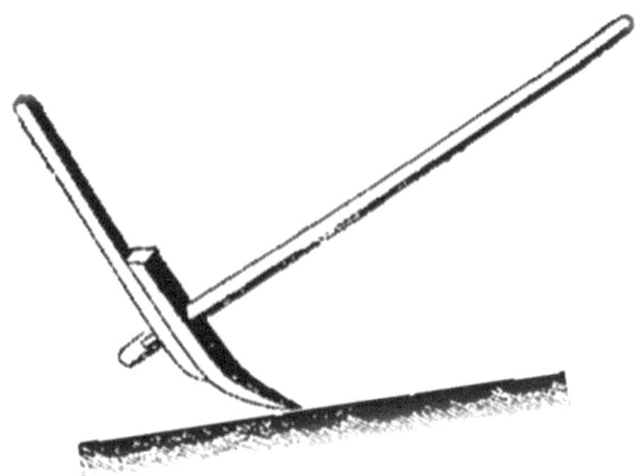

19. A Single-Ploughed, Ploughman!

When we read the poems

sung by the Tamil [6]*Sangam* poets,

We thought that

they are *Atchaya Pathiram*

those itself,

turned as our begging vessels!

We are imprisoned

Not in the Ashoka Forest, but in the Ayodhi itself!

The ruling Rama's

only protect their designation-Sita alone!

They make sure that

vote legs of their

'Throne-cot' is not broken!

---

[6] Assembly of the highly learned people of the ancient Tamil land

Who will come to listen

and rescue us from this prison?

We are

single-ploughed farmers

No other way!

For those of us

who lives with 'Tamil' in heart,

What is the way-source to live in Tamilnadu?

We have armed letter (௸) though

not to attack, but even

unable to defend ourselves!

Our Tamil people,

from lips-ship

slowly

imported the Tamil language and are

exporting other languages.

Oh, Tamil mother...

We are in praise exporting you

but no one respects us!

You are clad in *Semmozhi* silk

the life of many of your children

Neither get any line-shape,

nor get any light form!

20. Government Job Chance

All the birds are wavering

to build a nest at Ficus tree,

A few birds have lost their

feathers quite before that!

A day before the interview,

there happening a search

to see the roots of money-tree!

On the day of the interview, for many people,

life has become a mere mirage!

Even if Valluvar comes,

not even an Iota of doubt,

It is only the rich will win!

Although

the great educationist Kamban comes,

they will stop

and make him to stand outside by saying that

"You neither have a certificate nor a [7]key ticket."

---

[7] Money

Even if Saraswathi (Goddess of Education) and
Thirumagal (Goddess of Wealth)
go for the interview,
Only Thirumagal will get the job!
Saraswathi must return with a
kind of confusing-glared eyes!

Hundreds of thousands of hands
are stretching for Government job-flower.
Hands with Lakhs alone plucked
that job-flower!

Without breaking the hands of bribery,
there is no dawn for ambitious hands.

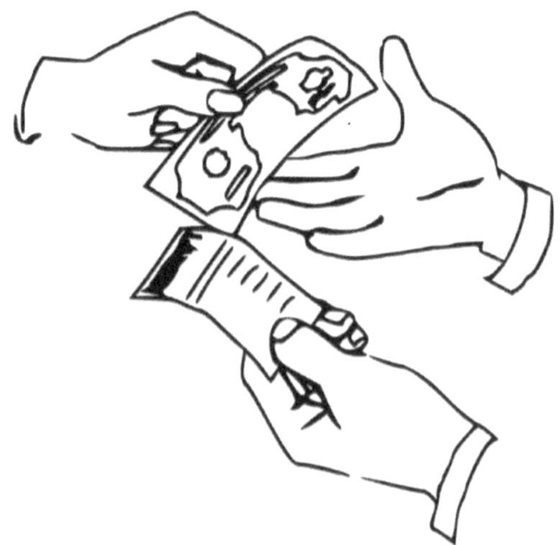

21. **Democratic leaders**

Leaders are sold

in the democracy's electoral market!

Those who are sold for highest bidder

is the ruling party!

Those who are sold for lowest bidder

is the opposite party!

They only meet the people

when this election market takes place,

People also meet them.

In this democratic lamp,

only darkness burns in all the four directions!

In daylight

leaders promise people.

It is only at night, people

make their promise for their vote!

Even people prefer protection of their leaders
more than the people!
To wipe the sweat of leaders,
'they' will shed even their blood!

If leaders go to jail,
'they' will prey on society.
'They' will turn public properties
as an asset of fire and will stain them!

Match-stick won't lit
while frictioning even to lit the lamp,
But it will lit up immediately
for the leaders!
Right from [8]Kannagi's period,
this fire is having this same job!

---

[8] A legendary Tamil woman who forms the central character of the
Tamil epic *Cilapathikaram*.

Fingers which Plucks the Star

Chastity-fire (Kannagi)

commands the fire to fire,

That loyal-fire excluded

children, chaste women, and elders

and burnt all the rest.

Today's fire burns everyone!

Where's that fire available?

If Kannagi were here,

can hear from her about this.

People have the democratic right

to choose

which leader has to come and plunder,

once in five years!

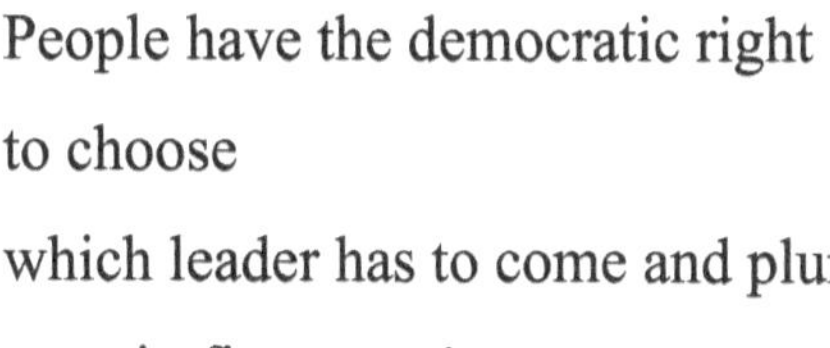

On the day of election,

Index finger will have the black-ink,

But democracy, itself will coat black-ink,

in its face!

22. **Memories of Stepped Down into Fire**

I have loved you

that's why I stand at the

door of your heart!

You have read me

that's why you have moved on

to the next page of life!

I know your legs will walk pretty,

I have never dreamed that

those would pass me by!

You gave me love-boon.

But why?

You held up another person's hand!

Oh! Tender vine…my mind's pole is

messed up without you!

> Dream-shop-spread eyes of mine
> now doing protest!
> With pretending inner mind,
> to get married,
> how have you got down my thought-Sita
> into the fire?

23. Consonantal Vowel

You, a man of sterling character!
Since you were a characteristic-word,
there are many words loaded as a
meaning of your truth!

You were holding a cane,
India holds 'you' as a cane!

The lands where your cane touched,
were bloomed non-violence flowering plants!

What we are holding securely

is not your policy card,

your smiling face on rupees note!

Truth test has happened to you,

We also will be tested,

while figuring out a rupee-note

whether it is fake or not?

You reduced your dress, indeed,

wore the dress of principles.

We follow you in our outfits but

we are nude in our principles!

Is this Gandhi's nation?

Or our fake makeup notion?

Oh! Fake sticks...

Hold the truth-stick,

before the rebirth of our man with a stick.

Once again, a non-violence war will come!

Not against the white people

but against a few white-clad people!

24. **Fish-they-are, fishermen!**

Our

Tamil fishermen

fell down as

'Fish-they' are

in Sri Lanka's Net!

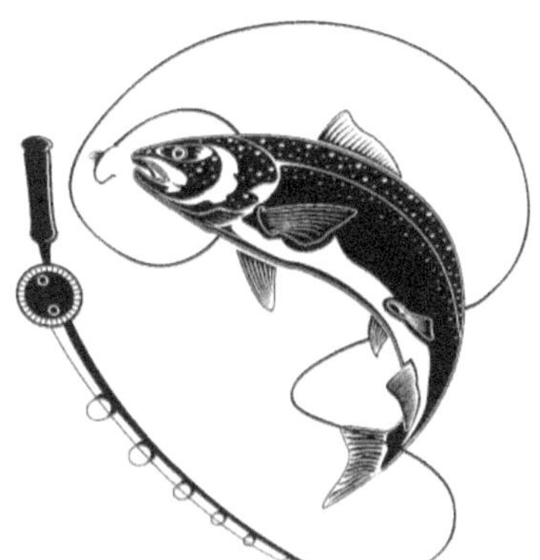

25. **The Habit of Smoking**

Don't tell them as

smokers anymore!

They are just holding cigarettes,

Only those who are next to them

inhale that smoke!

26. Caste-fire

Nobody should catch caste-fire,

If you hug it up,

We, will sink-head to get rid of you.

27. Alcohol Exclusion

Before the family lights

turned into dark houses,

Abolish alcohol!

28. The Youthful Bait

Her eye-fishes has spread the web

My youthful bait getting trapped!

29. Hill Circumambulation

Among the people who have come

to the full-moon hill circumambulation...

A full moon is revolving around the hill!

I turned as a hill, circumambulating the moon!

30. The Voice of God

"Lord, protect me!"

A devotee prayed.

The voice of God heard from the Sanctum

"Dear devotee, save me,

In the morning they are going to smuggle me!"

31. **Lines**

They are not living by putting a line,
they are living within the lines!

They are not chaste-women
who never cross the step.
They are the people of starvation
who can't cross the line!

Those lines are indestructible
by any eraser!

It is those who went to the fort
by saying that "I can erase this line"
made the line still stretching!

Which Lakshman drew this line?
Our poverty-Sita wasn't able to
jump-over this line!

Oh, Ruling parties...
What response you are going to tell
to poverty, the opposite party?

Poverty, India's first party,
without a leader,
Started by a few hoard-leaders,
a party with more members!

Poverty is prospering and prosper is in poverty!
In our growing nation,
if the poverty line is eliminated,
then, new directions will be visible!

32. **Hope**

If you fall down, fall down like a seed,
there is no downfall for you!

If you expand, expand like the sky,
there is no boundary for you!

33. **Rama who does not Get Sita**

I thought that young Dasaratha (Rama)
would marry me.
Within it, life-Kaikeyi has sent me into exile!

Family burden fell as a heavy garland
on my shoulders which are awaited
for wedding garlands!

For my sister's *Kalyani* raga,
I sang *Mukari* raga to my youth.
For my brother's aims
I burned myself as an oil-lamp!

Among my family characters
I'm an axial character (*Atchaya Pathiram*)

I walk as a character of hope for my family,
walking with hope as a characteristic utensil!

Although the flowers of my age are withered,
the roots of hope weren't withered!

Any longer a companion is not needed in my life.
Oh life! At least will you come
as a companion to my life?

34. The Migrating Moon

Who said there were no lives on the moon?

without knowing the fact that my life is in you!

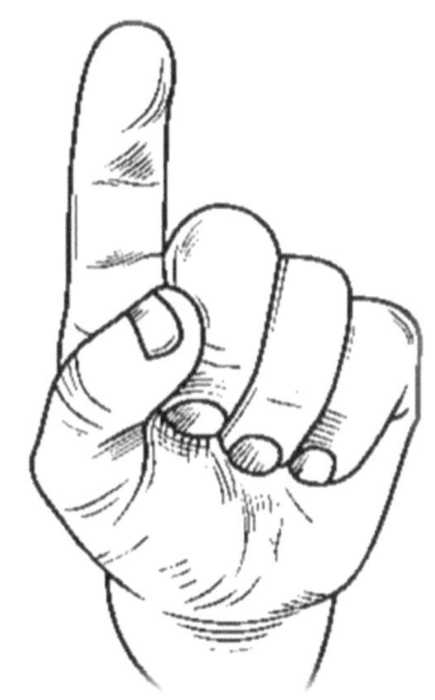

35. Lips

Being the eyes of this nation and

shed tears for this nation are no more needed.

Hereafter, let us pronounce like the lips and

warn those who ridicule us!

36. **Representative of Fingers**

You run to show the next person,

you will only cover your grievance.

People call you as index-finger!

You not only point people,

Once in every five years,

you are the one who shows up even the rulers!

You are the reason

for so many peoples to get positions but

We don't even offer a ring-position to you!

You are not tempted for the positions.

You choose the person

who wants the post - and then

you get all the fingers together

and get the money!

Other fingers send you alone to cast the vote!

You are the representative of the fingers,

electing the representatives of people!

37. **Road Will Write the Rule**

The fate will be written on the road

for those who do not respect

the written road rules!

38. **Lights Which Never See the Dawn**

We locked you in grammar handcuff,
We preyed you as a beast!

You are the shrine with sanctum,
instead of praying you,
we made you spin
around us like a temple!

Although half of the body has given
we are on the right side of strength
we just gave you space just on the left side!

We'll set you fire but
we'll name your name to the rivers!
We'll be keeping up the boons and
will give you curses as boons.

We will take out your rights and
yet will celebrate Women's Day!

To our eyes your physical beauty is visible
but the cry of your heart won't be visible to us.
You are always being a shortened sound
that is why we are sounding lengthy and stretchy!

The world was known to us only because of you,
but your world is concealed within us!

Oh,
She...used to wake up at the dawn!
Rise up a dawn for you too!
These roosters do not voice for your dawn
They'll be crowing for your sunset!

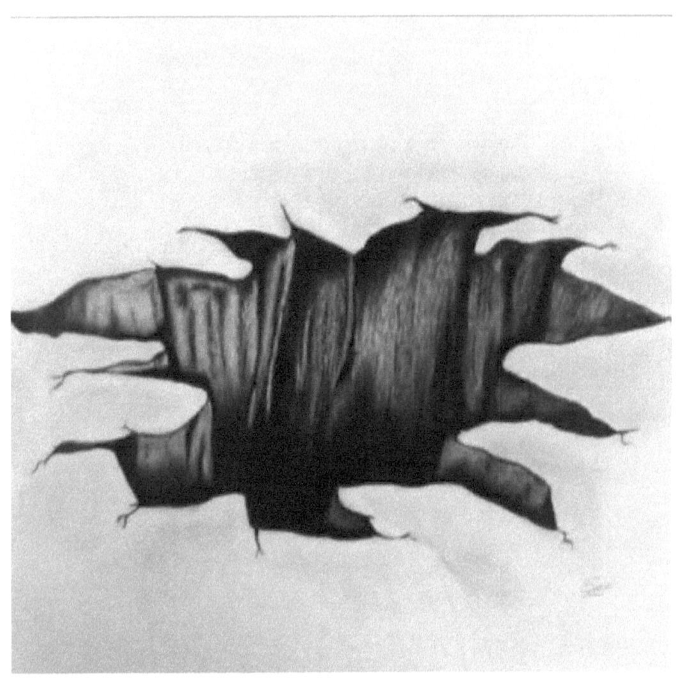

39. For what?

The roads in our towns

are itself rainwater harvesting tanks!

Then why do we need them at homes?

40. **Nature**

Human has broken the nature's hand
and is living with an artificial hand!

Like his mind, human has polluted the air,
then he has monetised
the cultivation lands into cash lands.

The breast of the Earth had dried up
because he had breast-fed the water!

Rolled the next generation as dice
This Dhuchadhana's had striptease
the Earth's natural clothes!

Forgetting gratitude is your nature.
That's why have you forgotten the
gratitude of nature?

Oh, human join your hands with nature.
Don't spoil the nature by joining the hands!

41. **Social Change**

On that day
Individual fought for the society
Today
Society is struggling vigorously for the individual!

42. **Let's thrown out the White Screen**

This white screen darkens the mind and

feasts the light to the eyes!

For the sake of entertainment

it has ruined the lives of many young people.

It is to shed sweat while working,

why they are sweating in theatres?

A slim waist is a beauty just,

For actresses, clothes are even

minimal than the waist!

The primitive man
would not have been weaved clothes
if he knew that the clothes
will be obscene like this.

Even if Gandhi arrives,
the actor who disguised as Gandhi will be celebrated
because here disguises have become reality,
the realities have turned just disguise!

Fan goats are chopped in theatre butcher shops!
The whites did not leave the country.
Still, they're ruling us through this white screen!

Only if this white screen just quit,
morning star will sprout into the
lives of young people!

43. **Omen**

A cat has come out,

On seeing a man on the opposite side,

it went back to the inside and feel

embarrassed that the omen was not right!

44. **Orphanage**

Many homes are orphaned,

because of the homes for aged are increased!

45. For what this Evolutionary Growth?

How could man appear from the monkey?

The elements of the monkey are not even little!

What has been the use of your evolution?

Evolution has robbed out

love and compassion and have locked humanity!

By the confluence of two false bodies,

human animals leave the baby orphaned!

You're the one has to be in the zoo, aren't you?

46. Our Tamils

Evolved are our foes here

on seeing the disunity of Tamils!

47. The Nation of Tears

We, sank heads in the rivers,

 in the past.

The rivers itself gave head-sank to the water,

at present!

Groundwater has dried up and given a heavy blow.

Just without water

the agriculture dye has gone.

So that the eyes of peasants

sank into the tear sea!

Our water nation has become a nation of tears!

48. The Plough-man

Crop writings by him -

are life writings of the world!

The fields were raised the paddy beads

with the sweat sprayed by him.

He who sowed the fields

to chase Hunger - the national integrity,

was buried in poverty!

Indian mother's crops, the silk clothes

are burned about.

The one who ran plough ran in search of a job!

49. **Bundle-lifting Workers**

Are these kids are going to

Calvary hill named as schools

by carrying Book-crosses!

Instead of questioning in knowledge

education has turned their spine

into a question mark!

At the age of playing with peacock feathers

which are kept in the books,

As broken-winged birds,

children were trapped

like peacock feather between the books!

Is it okay to load so many books,
in these baby carts?

This baby *Veena*s have turned wood timber
as of playing tragic-tunes instead of ragas!

These sugar mills squeeze the tender sugarcane kids,
Who named these mills as schools?

Education has created these children as just
bundle lifting workers, hasn't it?

50. **Wind**

What does the wind say?

Trees shake their heads!

51. **Solidarity/ Integrity**

Why your legs had broken

Which been come in running?

What is happening in Kannada?

We expanded our eye-flowers for you,

Oh! Cauvery...would you come?

But by spreading hands' you said no!

We are singing Conical-line (*Kanal Vari*).

Water has drawn these lines,

When these timelines will change for Tamils?

Fingers which Plucks the Star

At the time of writing the laws of water - Tamils

have written the tears as their fate!

Who does not solve our thirst then

what is the benefit of talking brotherhood

to you, Kannadians'?

In this guise of integrity,

the land is slowly and slowly weary of water!

52. **Have been Losing my Sleep…**

When you just walk down the street,

my mind celebrates the festival.

My mind chariot is rolling behind you

when your eyes are pulling the rope-cord!

There are many sweet notes

rise from the music of your ankle chain.

Any music that falls into my ears

only falls as the music of your ankle chains!

Fingers which Plucks the Star

You read these love poems
which I wrote about you like these,
You have torn them and
thrown them at your feet!

I am happy with that too, because
that's where the poems were born!

She, the originator of
modern poems in me,
Living as a conventional poem!
I, without being able to forget you,
have been losing my sleep!

53. **Thieves**

Be aware

Nowadays thieves

do not come by breaking the roof tiles,

They are getting in by being bought the votes!

54. **Umbrella**

Trees are Umbrellas spread open by the Earth

for just getting drenched!

55. Stars - the Ornamental Dots

Night, laid those star dots,

to draw a decorative figure!

but Sun's hands have scattered those dots!

56. National Tree

What happened to this Banyan tree?

It grows beard and stands alone like this!

57. Revolution

Over the clouds gathered in the sky road,

thunder bombs fell,

lightning batons flowed.

The clouds wept and poured

the blood rain down on the soil.

58. Garland

Kathiravan (sun) stepped off

the sky platform

at a fast pace,

Soon after garlanding westward direction!

59. **Today**

Raman had been feeling sorry after the wedding…

"Did I break the bow for this Soorpanagai?"

60. **Memento**

I gave her a memento.

She leaves me

by giving her memories as a memento!

61. **Society**

We are gathered together,

Live in one place separately!

62. **New Moon**

Oh, moon!

Why do you run around

with a black towel over your face?

Oh!

Can't you repay the light-loan from the sun?

63. **Search**

I was looking for material all my life,

By losing the meaning of life!

64. **Difference**

Musth catches the elephant.

Human catches the religion!

65. **1947**

Independent India purchased in the dark

has been still keeping in the dark by them,

to facilitate robbery!

66. Oh, Sea! A Few Questions to You…

Sea-She has always been staring at the sky mirror,

I'm throwing some question nets at you…

Are these waves that are keep on touching your

shore-husband are the forearm borders (*Munthaanai*)

of your blue saree?

Or else

Are you spitting on the shore

that keeps holding you back?

Or

Foam caused by washing your blue saree?

They are respected as fishermen
because they donate your fish eyes!

Even though pearl children are growing in your
stomach,
why are you getting troubled
by carrying with the boat baskets in your head?

For the questions, I have asked,
Something is being said aloud,
by your wave-mouth.
I can't understand what you are saying
like the leaders of our nation!

67. Leaders Who Came to the Street

Gandhi Road,

Nehru Road,

Kamarajar Street,

Anna Road…

All these leaders have come to the street!

Their policies are flying up in the air in the nation!

68. Today's [9]*Paari*'s

Those Jasmine vines,

that have no way to grow,

are being asked

to bring a car, to bring chariot,

by the Pari's of today!

---

[9] Pāri, one of the seven philanthropists of *Sangam* era, known as the one who gave his chariot to a climber plant.

69. **God's Fear**

Oh, dear Humans,

You have kept the letters safely

which I have sent to you, but,

you have thrown away the messages in it!

You worship the messengers

whom I have sent, but,

you have broken away

the message tiles that they have brought!

I told to keep flower shops, but,

you were running the butcher shops!

I told you to wipe tears, but,

you became the reason for tears!

I told you to be a medicine, but,

you have found the wounds!

I told you to grow up humanity, but,

you have grown up the religions!

One has interrupted the God, who was speaking,
"Which religion's God you are?"

God said, "I'm beyond religions."

The man told him to join his religion.

God was scared and ran away that he himself
will be caught by religion!

70. **Inside Outside**

The Gods with dried stomach and torn clothes

are outside the temple.

The idols inside the temple have special worship!

71. **The Holy Book**

The holy book of religions can be anything

The holy text of human is *Thirukkural*!

72. Forgetfulness

I'm having always forgetting something.

The thing which always remains

without forgetting is Oblivion!

73. Power

Can authority (*Athigaram*) conquer the World?

Can

Only by the *Thirukkural*!

74. **Let us Celebrate Humanity**

O man of the whole world,
Is it right for you to be an alien to yourself?

Countries will be won by wars,
You are defeated, aren't you?
You have put yourself defeated down, but,
you're telling that you were won!

Man, come out of the blanket of wars!

You only know just to love the nation?

Don't you know how to love you?

You are

Not an Indian

Not an American

Not Japanese

You are human!

Come on, humans!

We will pay tears tribute to the weapons,

in the borders.

Let us throw away the lines from the world map.

Let us give birth to anew.

There, day by day we will celebrate humanity!

75. Food and Stomach

The stomach is waiting for the food in poor homes

Food is waiting in the comfortable people's homes!

76. *Cilapathikaram* is Still Reverberating

The story of the Gold winning over the smile!

Kannagi's tears – the story about

the burnt of Madurai.

With the witness of the town

they began the family life.

He on seeing Maadhavi – family life

bent like a bow!

She danced over the stage – he got down

in her beauty!

Her art of dance – scattered his masculinity.

He, gave her a gift,

for her art of dance – a *Manimegalai*.

He lost all his wealth at Maadhavi.

However

With smile, Kannagi has accepted him, why?

She thought that her wealth is Kovalan, who has

returned to her, is that thought?

Kannagi's smile – gave comfort to him –

when she showed her ankle ornament, he got hope.

He called Kannagi to Madurai – without knowing
that fate is calling him to Madurai!

The King of Madurai
– found him as a thief – slew Kovalan.

Kovalan stole two ornaments, not one!

By being with Maadhavi
stole Kannagi's ornament-smile,
By rejoined with Kannagi
stole Maadhavi's ornament-smile!

Kannagi heard the news of Kovalan's death.
She asked the justice to Nedunchezhiyan.
In the pearl land of Pandiyan,
Kannagi broke the rubies.

Nedunchezhiyan by his small act became
Short-chezhiyan!
The one who hailed justice as his eyes – has ended
up, with the world's mock.

Kannagi's chaste fire
– turned Madurai, into the prey of fire -
wiped away the thief-stain of her husband.

It never ended up with
the *Vanchi Kaandam*[10]– in the life of many women –
still, *Cilapathikaram* is reverberating!

---

[10] *Cilapathikaram* (the Tale of an Anklet) a classical epic has three
division, Vanchi Kaandam is last division.

77. **River**

It is

the funeral rally of the water!

78. **Stars**

Cloud smoke hiding the eyes,

The 'day' cooked in the Sun oven,

So that, in the sky-pot

overflowing those star rice morsels!

79. **Beauty**

I stacked up the things scattered by the child.

The beauty in the scattering is not in the stacked!

80. **Fingers which Plucks the Star**

Are you born, just to lament?

You, analyse yourself,

The new refreshing light is visible!

Worries are not fingers,

They are nails, just chop!

Your fingers have the power

to pluck up even the star.

Thou, crying for dirt on nails!

Why do you dim your eyes,

at the thorns on the road?

When you reach your place,

those who thrown thorns on the road

will be waiting with Rotana flowers!

This world –

if it knows you are walking –

will throw thorns on the track.

If it knows for sure that you can't walk,

will shower flowers at your funeral procession!

Don't worry about the world!

Create a world which worries,

if something happens to you!

Tell the Sun that, you too have a sun, inside!

On seeing your energy,

let the wind also learn,

let the storm also afraid and run away!

81. An Exit Exam for the Poor!

Her neck, where the stethoscope should hang
was hanging in the gallows rope!

Her eye-lamps nurtured with dreams
were turned off in seconds,
Because of this entrance exam!

'NEET' exam why turned as a
'Neat' stretched rope?

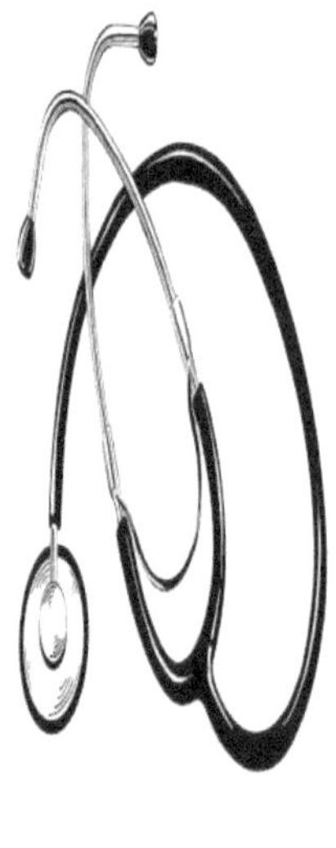

She would have thought that

her score would lift her up,

Would she have thought that it will hang her?

Death is readily available for the common man.

Only medical care is not easily available for them!

O... Those who have entered through elections,

This is not an entrance exam,

but an exit exam for the poor!

82. **Sea**

It is the

tomb of water!

83. **Guard Your Tongue**

O... With the tongue of leaves

the trees that speak the wind language!

Your tongues are fell down, there at your roots.

"Whoever be it, guard your tongue," Valluvar said,

It is not just for us, it's for you too!

84. **Thanks for the Shower**

What is this?

Is the sky is singing a lament song

for the missing Sun?

Are the clouds are performing

a water war, over the Earth?

We made one who comes for the livelihood, to live.

We have provided a place to stay,

for the rainwater too, inside the house!

The thunder hit our hearts,

It was rained in our eyes,

tears were mixed with the rain!

If it rains, the tree will sprout in our land.

For the first time humanity sprouted.

The rain will shower equally,

This rain has equalised everybody,

Let us thank this rain! (Chennai Flood 2015)

Humanity

85. Flowers Blooming Poems of Mu. Metha

One who owned all the words -
Communism speaking modern poet.

Although living in the mansion,
this great poet sings
without forgetting the smell of mud hut!

Black as ink - but your pen's ink
is the seed of light!

Police stations are not the first
to file F.I.R for crimes,
It is your poems filed them first.

In the white sheet cradle -
your poem-baby crying is for
the wounded hearts!

Metha's poems are always blooming for the poor,
until the day when human remains in the soil!

Mu. Metha

86. **Great Pongal**

The crowd which used to gather for the sea,

for the first time gathered as a sea!

Those who went to see the tomb only,

today, stepped feet in the beach

to save the culture from becoming mausoleum!

The lesson was taught by students

who used to listen to the lessons!

Not just memorising

we know our ethnographic lesson too,

they took and spoke!

Occasionally the sea will surge up,

Entire Tamil clan has grown high in this day,

It is not just Pongal, a Great Pongal indeed!

Glossary:

1. *Atchaya Pathiram* - inexhaustible vessel
2. Ettayapuram - birth place of the revolutionary poet Subramaniya Bharathiyar
3. Mausoleum -   tomb
4. Rotana - jasmine flower
5. *Semmozhi* – classical language
6. Valluvar - Thiruvalluvar a well-known Classical Tamil poet
7. ஃ - *Aaytha ezhuthu* is a unique and special character to Tamil language and script.